FARM ANIMALS

Peter Partington

HarperCollins*Publishers*

First published in 1996
by HarperCollins Publishers
London

© HarperCollins Publishers 1996

Editor: Diana Craig
Art Director: Pedro Prá-Lopez, Kingfisher Design Services
DTP/Typesetting: Frances Prá-Lopez, Kingfisher Design Services
Contributing artists: John Davis, Robert R. Greenhalf, Martin Hayward-Harris, Roger Hutchins

A catalogue record for this book is available from the British Library

ISBN 0 00 412790 0
Printed by Midas Printing Ltd in Hong Kong

CONTENTS

Introduction

Farm animals are familiar and much-loved inhabitants of our rural landscape. Once roaming free in migrating herds, these wild creatures were domesticated by early man. Since then, they have provided us with many of the comforts we take for granted, such as meat, milk, and clothing. They have also given us much more – rich and varied subject matter for legend and folklore, song and story, painting and sculpture.

Rural art

The farmers who raised these animals were proud of their achievements and often wanted pictorial records of their stock. Landowners, too, wanted paintings of their new breeds, and out of these trends grew a rural art. In the eighteenth century, Dutch painters depicted peaceful pastoral scenes of cows and sheep. Victorian artists did likewise, sometimes adding turbulent weather to their scenes of Highland cattle.

Even in today's industrialized countryside, there is plenty for us to draw. On the whole, farm animals are reasonably accessible. There are city farms run by local councils, and rare-breed farms which welcome visitors. Cattle and sheep can often be drawn from the vantage point of roads and footpaths, and many people still keep chickens. Farmers are friendly folk on the whole and, with prior permission, will allow artists to draw in yard and barn.

The Countryside Code

Always observe the Countryside Code. When you draw the animals, try to disturb them as little as possible. Always ask permission before you enter private property. Take home your litter, and shut gates after you. Good drawing!

Tools and Equipment

For the beginner artist, the huge range of drawing materials available may seem both exciting and daunting. All can be used to capture the diversity that farmyard life presents to us, but each tool does create a slightly different effect and mood, so some may be better suited than others for conveying the impression of a particular animal. When choosing your materials, the trick is to try out different ones and see which produces the most effective results for the drawing you have in mind.

Pencils

The everyday pencil is one of the most versatile of all drawing instruments, capable of producing rough, quick sketches as well as finely worked detail. Pencils come in various degrees of hardness, and it is this that affects the quality of line. The H range, ending with the super-hard 9H, creates a light, precise line ideal for careful studies of eyes, fur and feather. The

soft B range, culminating in the luxurious 9B, can provide rich, rough, textural effects and striking tonal variations. Midway between the hardness of the H range and the softness of the B range is the well-known HB all-rounder.

Some people prefer specialized pencils, such as clutch and propelling pencils. These come in a lower range of softness, but do not need to be constantly sharpened in order to produce a continuous and consistent line.

Coloured pencils enable you to draw and introduce colour simultaneously, while watercolour pencils produce a line which can be softened with a wash of water.

Explore the range of pencils by using as many different types as possible to discover what effects they produce and which suits your intentions and feelings best.

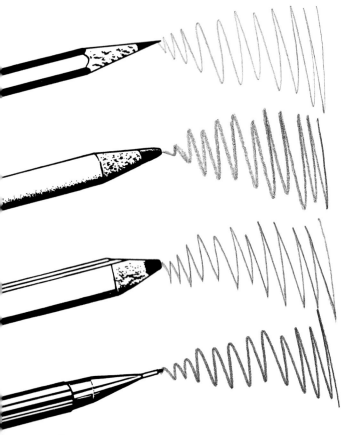

The rich texture of a black wax pencil conveys the rotundity of this cockerel dusting itself in the sun.

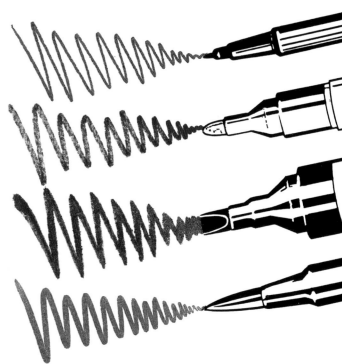

The softness of the down on these chicks was conveyed with the fine point of a ballpoint pen.

Overlapping strokes, a technique known as cross-hatching, were used to build up the tones.

Pens

Pens can produce a fluid, uncompromising line. They are available in several varieties, which produce slightly different effects and so are suited to different uses.

Fountain and **dip-pens** allow the artist to draw free-flowing or angular lines which vary in thickness depending on the pressure applied.

Ballpoint and **technical pens** produce a consistent, fine line. They are useful for sketching moving animals because they are quick to apply.

Felt-tip pens, in a range of widths, can create a similar effect, depending on their nibs.

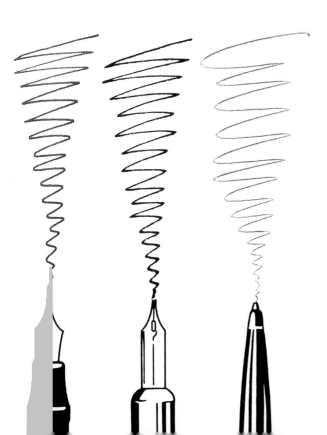

Artist's Tip

Make sure you replace the tops on your felt-tip pens or the nibs may dry out. Wash out dip-pens after using or the ink will become encrusted on the nib.

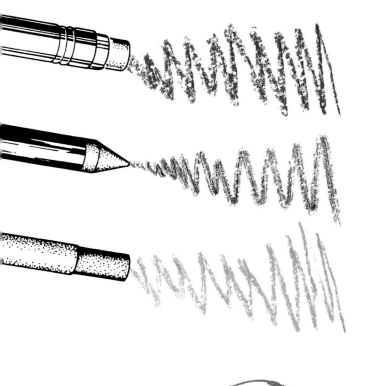

Pastels, crayons and chalks

The soft, textured quality of pastels and chalks offer an exciting alternative to the precision of pencils and pens. They work best on rough papers. The rich, powdery marks and lines which they produce can be smudged and blended. They are ideal for conveying the depth of thick fur or the sheen on a glossy coat because you can work light over dark, or allow the coloured paper base to show through.

Pastels and **chalks** can be used on their tips or on their sides to fill large areas quickly. Their rough, unfocused line can suggest light, movement and mood. They are particularly effective for lively, spontaneous drawing.

Oil pastels and **wax crayons** come in a dazzling array of colours, and allow you to introduce colour at the same time as line and contour. Soft oil pastels can be built up to resemble oil paint, but take care not to overwork wax crayon. Plan your picture carefully before you begin because these 'greasy' media are difficult to erase.

Oil pastel was used to sketch this simple sheep shape. By varying the angle at which you hold the pastel, you can create different densities of line.

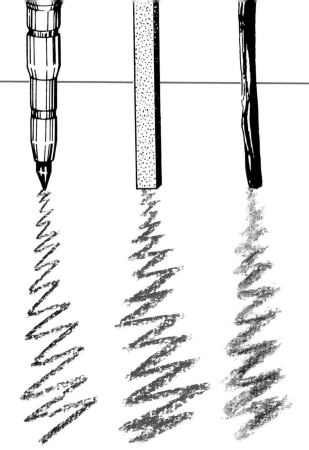

Conté crayon is similar in quality to pastel, but its slightly greasy texture makes it harder and less crumbly.

Charcoal traditionally comes in stick form. The softness of stick charcoal makes it perfect for working on a large scale, but it is rather messy, and drawings using this medium can easily become overworked. Charcoal is also made in compressed, pencil form for ease of handling. It produces a similar effect to the non-compressed variety but is more manageable if you wish to do smaller-scale work. To achieve a fine line with charcoal, gently rub the tip on sandpaper to produce a point.

Compressed graphite sticks look like large-scale pencil 'leads'. They come in various softnesses, and produce effects that resemble generous pencil strokes. They are a good tool to use if you want to work quickly, building up your drawing with a large number of lines.

To pick out highlights in a pastel or charcoal drawing, dab the surface with a putty eraser, or blend colours by rubbing them with your finger.

This young donkey's head was drawn in black chalk, which offers the rich, vibrant tones and soft textures that are perfect for the animal's hair.

Artist's Tip

Charcoal smudges easily, so avoid resting your hands on your drawing while you are working. When you have finished, spray fixative on the drawing. This is available in cans or bottles, or may be blown on through a blowpipe.

Brushes and wet media

As well as adding colour or tone to a drawing, certain wet media, such as ink and watercolour, can also be used for drawing the lines that define form and outline. Depending on the type of brush they are applied with, they can produce a variety of line – delicate and flowing, short and broad, long and rhythmic.

The type of line you can create is determined by the shape of the brush tip, and tips come in a wide range of shapes and lengths. Among the most useful brushes for drawing are those that have long, pointed tips, the 'rigger' type being the longest. These produce long, fine lines. The length of the tips makes them very pliable, however, and they can be hard to control: brushes with short-tipped points are more manageable and can be used for fine detail.

1

2

1 These brush marks were made with *(from left to right)* a small, pointed brush; a flat brush; a large, pointed brush.

2 Watercolour tone can be progressively reduced by adding more water, as shown by these strokes using different dilutions.

3

5

4

6

3 For an even layer of strong watercolour, lay darker washes over a light wash while still wet.

4 To prevent colours 'bleeding' together, let the first layer dry before adding the next.

5 For a soft, smudgy effect, paint watercolour on to paper that has been slightly dampened.

6 Ink or concentrated watercolour on damp paper will spread into swirls and blotches.

Brushes with flat tips, either short or long, are the best type for covering large areas, or for producing extreme variations of line, in a similar way to a calligraphic pen.

The fibres or hairs used for brush tips vary in quality. Sable is the best-quality watercolour brush and gives very attractive results. Cheaper squirrel and synthetic fibres are quite adequate, however, and produce good-quality work. The tensile springiness of synthetic fibres can create fine, dynamic lines that are ideal for expressing the liveliness of certain animals. Brush-pens are good for this, too; they come supplied with a cartridge of coloured ink which ensures a consistent flow of colour.

Watercolour can be diluted with water to give transparent tones and gentle washes. For strong, vivid colours, reduce the amount of dilution.

Gouache is a form of watercolour that gives bold, opaque colour and dense coverage.

Acrylic paints can be diluted to create a watercolour effect; undiluted, they look like oils.

Ink may be applied with a pen to produce a line drawing, diluted and brushed on as a wash, or the two methods may be combined in a line-and-wash drawing – but do the underlying drawing with waterproof ink or the wash may cause it to 'bleed'.

For wet media, you will need a palette for mixing and a couple of jam jars – one containing water for mixing your colours, the other for washing your brushes.

A preliminary pencil sketch was strengthened with watercolour line, and overlaid with several quick washes, to produce this lively drawing of a Border Collie *(below)*.

Brush-pens are ideal for putting down an image quickly, as in this sketch of a sheep, characterized as a haystack shape with four stick-like legs.

Artist's Tip

When using wet media, change the water in your jar often so that it does not tint your colours. Test new colours by dabbing them on paper first.

Newsprint is a very cheap paper, and therefore ideal for practising and for doing rough sketches.

Tracing paper is semi-transparent and allows you to see through and trace images that you like.

Stationery paper, usually available in only one size, has a hard, smooth surface that suits the pen.

Cartridge paper is one of the most versatile of all surfaces. It usually has a slightly textured finish.

Surfaces to draw on

With experience, you will gradually learn which surface suits your style best, and which suits the medium you are working with. Try to experiment with different combinations of media and surfaces – it's exciting to explore the way in which each surface changes the appearance of each medium.

Watercolour paper is the most expensive paper you can buy. It may be made by hand or machine, and comes in different thicknesses that are measured according to the weight of a square metre. It is tough and absorbent, consisting partly or wholly of cotton and linen fibres which can give it an almost blotting-paper-like quality. It will withstand vigorous drawing and watercolour washes, and is acid-free so it will not go brown if left exposed to daylight.

Cartridge paper may be either cream or white, and is the most versatile, all-round surface for everyday drawing. You can buy cartridge paper in rolls or in sheets.

Soay sheep – a small and rare breed of sheep from the Scottish Isles – sketched with soft pencil on cartridge paper.

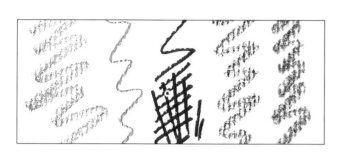

Ingres paper, with a lightly ridged surface, suits pastel and charcoal, and comes in various colours.

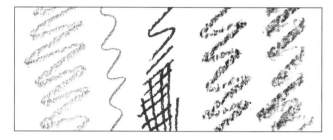

Watercolour paper is ideal for wet media, being thick and absorbent with a rough surface.

Bristol board is firm and has a smooth finish that makes it a very suitable surface for pen work.

Layout paper is a semi-opaque, lightweight paper that is good either for pen or pencil drawings.

The softness of 3B pencil on cartridge paper captures the velvety quality of this horse's head.

Cheap papers are another alternative. For example, the matt side of brown wrapping paper makes an interesting surface on which to work, as does photocopy paper and plain newsprint.

Blocks, **books** and **pads** are useful for outdoor sketching. Blocks are made of ready-cut and stretched watercolour paper on a card base. Books consist of watercolour or cartridge paper bound with a hard back. Pads are usually made of cartridge paper, spiral-bound or glued. They are available in two formats: *portrait*, or upright, and *landscape*, or horizontal.

Paper has three grades of surface: *hot-pressed* (smooth); *not* (not hot-pressed); and *rough* (textured). Smooth surfaces are best for pen and wash and detailed pencil work, while rougher surfaces suit bold work in pencil, charcoal or crayon. Pastels and chalks work best on special, textured pastel paper because their particles cannot cling to smoother surfaces.

Watercolour papers often have attractive textures – 'laid' or 'wove' – according to the mould they are made in. This can add enormously to the interest of your work.

Choosing the Right Medium

I

2

The final result you produce depends not just on the medium you choose, but also the surface on which you have been working – a particular medium may look different on different surfaces. Experiment with various combinations to see what kinds of results you can create, and which combinations best suit your style and subject matter.

You may, for example, want to portray the details in an animal, in which case a drawing tool with a fine point such as a hard pencil, applied to a smooth surface, will fulfil your aim. Alternatively, you may want to express a sense of flow and movement, or give a more general impression of the animal as a whole. Here, the flowing line from a wet brush on watercolour paper will enable you to convey this feeling more easily. To create a sense of mood and atmosphere, the softness of charcoal is ideal.

Looking at examples

The pictures on these pages show a cockerel in the same pose, yet all looking very different according to the medium and surface that has been used. Ballpoint pen on white card, as in the second drawing, for example, produces fine, crisp lines which are good for conveying the detail of fur, eyes, or feet. Compare this with the loose brushwork on wet watercolour paper or the charcoal on textured paper in drawings 4 and 5. The softness of these two combinations gives a sense of light, movement and mood.

From the examples on these two pages, you can see how, by exploring different combinations of medium and surface and then choosing the most appropriate, you can achieve the effect you want much more quickly.

I Soft pencil on cartridge paper
2 Ballpoint pen on white card
3 Dip-pen and ink wash on thick cartridge paper

4 Brush-pen on wet watercolour paper
5 Charcoal on textured paper
6 Watercolour on watercolour paper

3

5

4

6

Farm Mammals

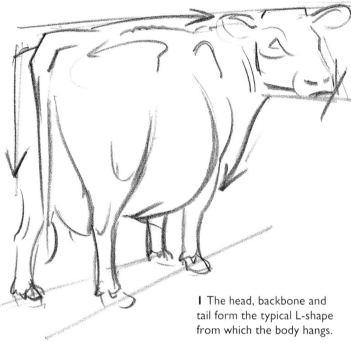

Cows, sheep, and pigs are the most familiar farm mammals and, of these, the milk-cow sums up all that is warm and secure in the farmyard.

Cows

The cow shown on this page is Kirsty, an Ayrshire – a breed which typifies the animal's angular 'wedge' shape that starts narrow at the front and widens out towards the rear, and provides a useful framework for your drawing. Here, the animal is seen from behind and the wedge is condensed. The full curve of the belly and rib-cage hangs down from the spine and the bony supporting limbs. The udder echoes this rhythm, and the tail provides a useful vertical.

1 The head, backbone and tail form the typical L-shape from which the body hangs.

2 I built up my initial sketch with charcoal to convey the body's roundness.

Head shapes

The shape of cows' heads varies, from the delicate and deer-like features of the Guernsey to the broad features of the great Charollais beef cattle from France. The little Guernsey has expressive brows, large black eyes, and a small nose; the Charollais, on the other hand, as you can see from the drawings below, looks altogether more robust.

When you draw this head, keep in mind its box-like form. Notice how the vertical sides of the cheeks almost form a corner as they meet the rather flat forehead and bridge of the nose. If you maintain this underlying structure as you develop your drawing, you will preserve the three-dimensional quality you need throughout the later stages of your cow 'portrait'.

1 I marked out the box-like structure lightly first, positioning the ears, eyes, and muzzle *(above)*.

2 I then worked into the drawing, suggesting the 'slab' sides of the cheek *(above right)*. I filled the eye with tone, leaving a white highlight.

3 Using a soft 8B pencil, I completed the drawing, indicating the curly top-knot and forehead as well as the crease-lines over the eye *(right)*. I then strengthened the whole head with more tonal marks, and left blank the shine on the nose.

Sheep

Gently grazing in green meadows, sheep form an essential part of the rural scene – and what typifies springtime more than new-born lambs?

There are many varieties of sheep, each having its own characteristics. The shape of each animal changes as the year progresses. The fleecy coat that develops towards winter makes a sheep's body appear more bulky, while still echoing the shapes of the limbs beneath. From beneath this bulk, the legs protrude like sticks. The thick collar of wool around the neck obscures its shape, so that head and body appear to merge. In early summer, however, the underlying structure of the animal's form is revealed when its woolly coat is shorn.

I Doing a drawing of a lamb feeding from a ewe is a good way to compare their different shapes. Here, I began by sketching in the basic outlines in pencil.

Notice how the ewe's body forms a square, with only the lower part of her legs protruding beneath, and how the head sits at an angle on the body.

2 I then rounded off the corners in my basic sketch, and drew sweeping curves to indicate the way in which the coat follows the form of the body underneath.

3 When I was happy with my basic drawing, I used Indian ink and a no. 3 pointed brush to draw the first strokes following the guidelines, and to begin picking out the lamb's shape from that of its mother. I then worked into the drawing with diluted ink, and white gouache paint.

Notice the slant of the almond-shaped eyes and the set of the ears, low down on the head, in this soft charcoal study *(above)*.

Looking at the head

As well as the differences in size, body shape and markings, the shape of a sheep's head varies from breed to breed. Some, such as the Suffolk, have a fairly short, triangular face; others, such as the Dorset, have a high-bridged 'Roman' nose; some breeds have larger eyes than others.

From the front, a sheep's head forms a long triangle. In all sheep, the eyes lie much closer to the ears than imagined, and the eye socket forms an important feature, its bold shape emphasized by a bony eyebrow ridge. Be sure to stress this circular form, and to fit the eye shape within it. The eye also has a pronounced tear duct flowing towards the nostrils, which are linked to the lips in a Y-shape within the small muzzle. On either side of the nostrils the muzzle swells out.

A sheep's ears are leaf-shaped, and have a connecting bridge to the muscles on the top of the head which control them. From the side view, the mouth has a slight 'smile', and the small nostrils hardly feature.

A half-grown sheep: the ears are still proportionately large and the nasal ridge is becoming prominent *(left)*. The long, curved nose, high 'raised' brows, and pinched nostrils can give a sheep a haughty look. I used an 8B pencil for this drawing.

Artist's Tip

If you are having difficulty drawing the ears, make a fake ear to study. Fold a piece of paper in half and cut out a leaf shape with the fold down the middle. Try drawing it end on and from other angles to give you confidence when drawing the real thing.

Goats

These animals have angular shapes that make them wonderful subjects to draw. They are closely related to sheep but are leaner and more gaunt, feeding as they do on marginal land. Because goats are more assertive than sheep, it may be wiser to draw that billy-goat from outside its enclosure!

Most breeds of goat look similar, although some, such as the Nubians, have floppy ears. Their bone and muscle structure can be very apparent.

Use your pencil marks to emphasize the goat's angular shapes. Work into the drawing gradually with marks that suggest hair lying over the form and around the cylindrical neck.

1 I began by sketching in the structure of the body with simple angular lines *(above)*. Notice how the feet align to indicate depth.

2 Next, I introduced detail with pencil strokes that follow the body hair, gradually darkening them and using cross-hatching to suggest form *(above right)*.

3 In my finished drawing, large brows emphasize the characterful head *(right)*. The horns flow out of the crown of the head as a natural extension.

Pigs

A popular subject for the artist, these animals are very accessible for drawing when confined to their pens. They come in a wide variety of breeds from the hairy Tamworth to the attractive Gloucester Old Spot. Here, I have drawn one of the breeds of 'black' pig.

Their shape is simple – muscles and bones are concealed by ample flesh. Begin with a bean-shape, drawing from the wrist. The legs are shaped like old-fashioned pegs, narrowing down from the hams to the points of the trotters.

The pig's nose may be seen as an upturned heart-shape which fits over the lower jaw and is punctured by its two nostrils *(above)*. Pigs have small eyes.

  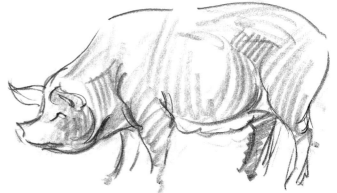

I To begin my pig, I drew loose, curving lines around the bean-shaped body, and suggested the upper hams

and rib-cage. Notice the 'S' shape of the jointed limbs. I hung the head and the ears from the front of the body.

2 Working in further, I began to add curving lines to suggest the body's weight and roundness *(above)*.

3 I completed the drawing in charcoal pencil to emphasize the form and hairy skin texture *(below)*.

Artist's Tip

Keep your hand flexible and draw freely from the wrist in order to produce rhythmic, flowing lines. You don't have to keep your pencil point sharp – a slightly worn head will give you a variety of thicknesses of strokes.

Horses

There are still a few farms that employ working horses, and you can also see them at county shows and at Shire horse centres. Their form reflects their amazing strength and spirit.

To draw a farm horse, begin by sketching a square, placing the barrel of the body in the upper half. From this, pull out the massive curve of the neck and head. Use the vertical of the tail to work out the curve of buttocks and hind legs.

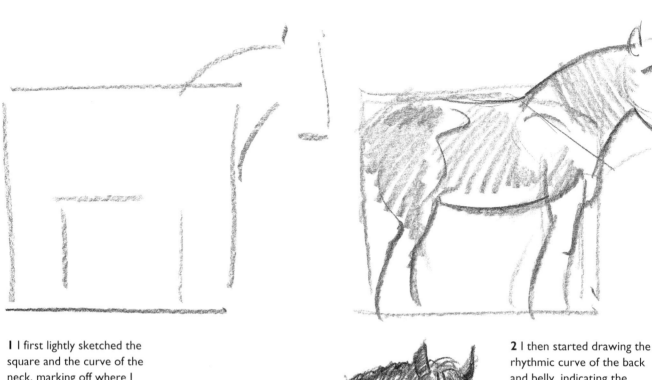

1 I first lightly sketched the square and the curve of the neck, marking off where I thought the head would be.

2 I then started drawing the rhythmic curve of the back and belly, indicating the width of the legs and suggesting how they link in with the body. The leaf-shaped ears and eye were added as markers.

3 Finally, to emphasize the contours of the body, I worked in tone with hatching strokes, leaving lighter areas for the gloss on the coat.

Rabbits

Wild and tame rabbits can usually be found about the farmstead. The tame ones come in many colours, shapes and sizes, from the giant Hollands and lop-ears to the miniatures.

When running, rabbits' bodies stretch out, but when sitting they retract into compact shapes like that of the rabbit below.

In side-view, a rabbit's head is almost a triangle, tilted slightly. The pointed end forms the small nose. The eye is large, and over it curls the large brow which can sometimes be seen to link up with the muscles that control the ear. The ears are roughly the same length as the head. Two leaf shapes can form the basis for ears. Your pencil strokes should imitate the directions taken by the fur itself.

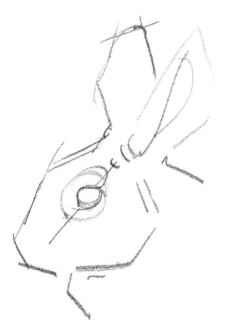

1 Two triangles, their points downwards, form the basic shapes of the rabbit's head and ears.

2 Working into the two triangles, I first drew the concentric circles around the eye, adding emphasis to the brow. I then worked into the eye, leaving a blank spot for the highlight.

3 To complete the drawing, I began to work in the tone, using my pencil strokes to follow and define the contours. Notice the lighter areas on cheek, nose and ear.

Artist's Tip

Use tone to convey an animal's three-dimensional form. Unworked areas left blank will appear to swell out, while darker areas will appear to curve away, and will add weight to the form.

In this drawing of a seated rabbit (*right*), notice how the body has become a series of concentric circles, and the head and ears a tear-drop shape.

Farm Birds

Hens, ducks and geese are the most common feathered inhabitants of the farmyard, the hen being probably the most familiar farm bird.

Hens

As with other farm creatures, the simplest way of drawing a hen is to look for easy geometrical shapes which underlie the complex feathering.

The wing joint is folded quite forward under the hackles (neck feathers), and you can link this up with the saddle in a long 'S' shape. The saddle and tail often bulge over the tightly folded wings, and the flank feathers bulge nicely, too, giving the whole a very satisfying shape. The sturdy legs begin on a line with the base of the tail, and end in strong feet, suited to scratching.

1 I drew in the geometrical shapes lightly to guide my lines later *(far left)*.

2 Here I added the 'S' shape of saddle and wings, and the beginnings of head, beak and legs *(left)*.

3 The completed hen shows the feathering which can be marked out, as here, with semi-circular gestures around the form. Denser feathered areas were built up with cross-hatching.

Artist's Tip

The feathers of some farmyard birds have elaborate patterning: don't let this distract you. Look for the underlying forms before paying attention to the feathers.

Doves were once
not just a decorative
addition to the farmyard,
but provided a source
of food. Simplicity is the
theme in this pencil and
watercolour wash drawing
of a resting dove.

Ducks

After the hen, the duck is probably the most familiar farmyard bird. There are various breeds of duck, in different shapes and sizes.

The breed I have chosen to show here is the Khaki Campbell. This flightless bird relies on its endearingly comic waddle to get itself around. Its tapering body begins with its elegant head and neck, gradually filling out towards its rounded rear, which is firmly placed on its short, strong legs and paddle-feet. In the pose shown here, you can see the striking 'S' rhythm running through its shape, which is given an extra fillip by the curly tail feathers.

1 Keeping my wrist loose, I drew sweeping lines to indicate the rhythms flowing over the head, down the body, and back up again.

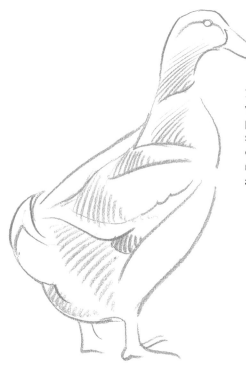

2 I added tone gradually with hatching strokes of my pencil. I used these lines to suggest contour and to describe how the feather masses wrap themselves around the body.

3 I completed my drawing by darkening certain areas to give weight and shape to the form – around the feet, under the tail feathers, and around the wings – varying the pressure on my pencil to create different thicknesses of line. I also strengthened the outline.

Geese

The domestic goose is similar in shape to the duck, and is descended from the wild Greylag. Some breeds are almost indistinguishable from their wild ancestor, while others are pure white or a mixture of the two.

Like that of the duck, the goose's body begins gracefully, but ends with a fat rear under the tail coverts. Its neck is long and can twist in a snake-like way. Its head is squarer than the duck's, and its bill more triangular, with a distinctive 'nail' on the end for cropping grass.

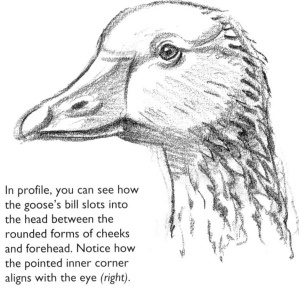

In profile, you can see how the goose's bill slots into the head between the rounded forms of cheeks and forehead. Notice how the pointed inner corner aligns with the eye *(right)*.

The goose has a long, elegant neck. From the base of the neck the body balloons out into a full, rounded form, slung low over the wide feet *(left)*.

The goose's neck feathers are pleated and fold into useful lines for describing movement. In some geese, the feathers are barred with the dun, scaly plumage of the wild bird, and these stripes provide an ideal opportunity for suggesting the roundness of the body. The big paddles of the feet give the bird a firm base.

Artist's Tip

Try to draw as much as you can from life. Even if your drawings are only sketchy, constant working from life will improve your grasp of the characteristics of each bird.

Structure and Form

Farm mammals are grass- and foliage-eaters. Grass takes a lot of effort to digest and it is the specialized digestive system of these mammals that gives them their characteristic bulk.

In the illustration below, you can see the massive rib-cage of the cow that contains the stomach and three other chambers, the largest of which is the 'rumen'. This contains bacteria which break down the woody content of the grass. The cow, like other 'ruminants', brings the grass up to chew it before finally digesting it.

Sturdy body
The cow's bones and muscles have to be very sturdy to support all this. The sinews join the muscles to the bones, and the muscles surround the tissues and bones to power the animal.

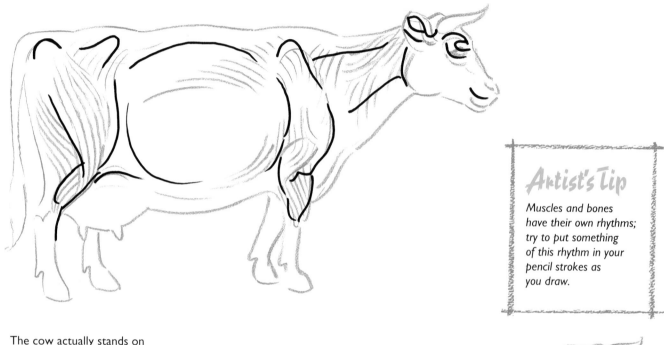

Artist's Tip

Muscles and bones have their own rhythms; try to put something of this rhythm in your pencil strokes as you draw.

The cow actually stands on its toes – the three-part bone structure enables the leg to fold easily and give good suspension. Observe the points at which the bones come close to the surface, and how this affects the surface shape *(above)*.

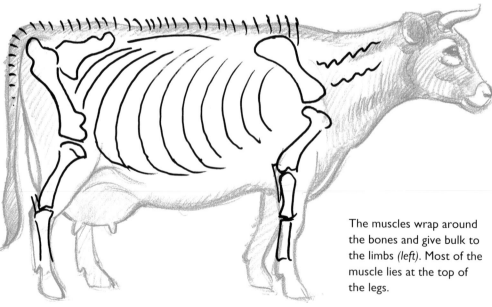

The muscles wrap around the bones and give bulk to the limbs *(left)*. Most of the muscle lies at the top of the legs.

Lambs are very active – the legs reveal the springy suspension system of the three-part bone arrangement in the limbs *(left)*. Their heads are big, and their necks are strong.

Flexible legs

Compare the bulky body of the cow with that of the lamb above. Lambs are not as yet weaned on to grass, so their belly has not yet developed a bulky digestive system.

What is more clearly apparent in this young animal, though, is the zig-zag structure of the legs which enables these mammals to compress and fold their limbs. The lamb can straighten its leg, or tense it ready to leap or run. The rear leg bends forward at the upper joint, like a human knee, giving dynamism to the animal's pose.

In resting posture, the front leg of the goat below is compressed and folded back, while the back leg stretches out forward. The other back leg will be folded under the body.

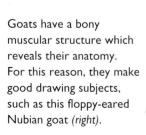

Goats have a bony muscular structure which reveals their anatomy. For this reason, they make good drawing subjects, such as this floppy-eared Nubian goat *(right)*.

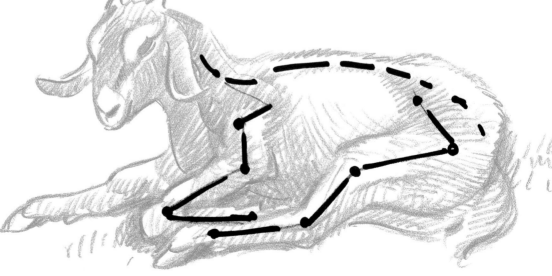

Feather masses

Of all farmyard birds the hen is the most familiar, and this is the bird I have chosen to look at here. The domestic hen is descended from various species of Asian jungle-fowl which have been imported into the West throughout history. From these stocks, various breeds have been developed by man, in an infinite range of colours and shapes.

Whatever the bird's size and shape, however, the basic plumage and anatomy remain the same. Once you understand something of the feather masses illustrated here, the birds become much easier to draw.

The bulk of larger feathers lies around the tail, the saddle and shanks. The feathers get finer and more compact up to the head, which appears small in relation to the body. You can see how the feathers tend to overlap each other, like roof-tiles, from the head to the rear.

Wings and tails

Hens' wings are small and tucked in. The 'shoulders' are held forward under the neck. The impressive tail display – the 'sickles' – of the cockerel are not in fact tail-feathers but well-developed upper tail coverts. These grow out from above the tail and are supported in their upright position by the tail-feathers themselves.

The more dominant the cockerel, the redder and larger his comb will be. This begins right above the beak, while the wattles begin under it, sometimes joining the flesh around the eye.

The cockerel stays alert so its upright stance is a natural aspect of its form *(left)*.

Underlying structure

The plumage of chickens conceals most of what is going on underneath. The leg muscles and bone emerge from the pelvis at the back of the knee, but this is totally concealed by feathers and lies close to the breast. The knee then joins the 'backwards' joint in an arrangement rather like that in the hind leg of a horse. The tarsus then appears from under the flank feathers, pointing forward to join the large scaly feet.

The bulk of the body lies over and ahead of the feet, which adds a forward momentum to the whole body. The wing bones are folded like an arm and tucked in under the neck. The neck itself is long and can be extended and contracted at will – the hackles (neck feathers) will expand and thicken the form as the neck folds back into the body of the bird.

The body of the hen is actually quite small under all its fluffy plumage *(above)*. The bird plants its feet in a straight line when it walks. Most of the bulk lies ahead of the feet, creating a rocking waddle.

Artist's Tip

The feather masses on chickens are often clearly defined by colour and tone. This makes them useful subjects for studying plumage.

Hackles, wing feathers and upper tail coverts mask the underlying structure of the hen *(left)*. Some breeds also have 'pantaloons' – bunches of feathers above the tarsus (ankle).

Proportion and Perspective

Your drawings of farm animals will have greater conviction if you get their proportions right. These vary, of course, from species to species, from breed to breed, and according to the age of the animal.

The effects of perspective

Although proportions remain constant in each animal, your viewpoint will change their appearance to the eye. For example, we all know that a cow further away will look smaller than one near at hand. This curious visual trick is called *perspective*, and can affect the proportions of an animal so that what you *see* differs from what you *know* – although you know that a cow has two pairs of legs of equal length, perspective may make the legs furthest away look shorter.

You can measure this visually, if necessary. The simplest method of doing so is to hold up a transparent ruler or lead pencil in front of your subject and mark the size of a part, say, the length of the head, with your thumb. You can then use this as your unit of measurement, and compare it with the size of other parts to check the animal's proportions. As your skills grow, your eye will begin to make these comparisons automatically, without mechanical help.

In the bull calf below, for example, you can see that its legs are still quite long in proportion to the body, and that its head is large. If you measure the length of its head, you will find that just over four 'heads' make up the length of the body. Similarly, its front leg goes into the length of its body about one and a half times.

I did this quick sketch of a bull calf rapidly with a soft-grade graphite stick.

Foreshortening

When you look at an animal from the front or rear, its parts 'telescope' together; this effect is known as *foreshortening*, and is illustrated in the drawing of young heifers below.

In this drawing, we are looking at these animals from in front and above – notice the distortions that occur. The bellies have almost disappeared, the rumps are higher than the heads, and the back leg of the heifer on the left starts level with the ears. Phenomena such as these are what you should be looking out for.

Seen from this viewpoint, the proportions of this cow *(above)* are extremely distorted, with a huge rear compared with a tiny head.

If you measured the heads of these heifers *(left)*, you would find that they are disproportionately larger than their bodies. However, our brains translate this distortion so that we 'read' their proportions as normal.

Different angles

The heads of farmyard animals – mammals, in particular – are formed of a fascinating series of curves, hollows, lumps and bumps. The rules of perspective come into play again here, affecting the shapes and proportions of eyes, ears, noses, and muzzles, depending on the angle from which you are viewing the animal.

When drawing an animal's head, it is very useful to use 'construction lines' – like the lines in the drawings below and opposite – to help establish the proportions of the various parts, and to site them correctly in the whole. As your skills improve, you will soon learn to visualize these lines without actually having to draw them.

Age differences

As with other parts of the body, the proportions of animals' heads vary depending on their age. In young animals, for example, eyes and ears tend to be larger in proportion to the rest of the head than in mature animals.

Your measurements will help to identify what age the animal is that you are looking at.

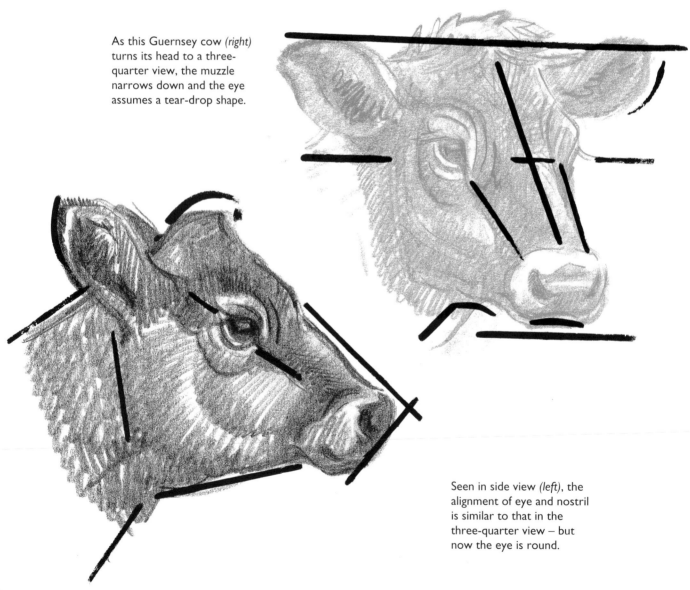

As this Guernsey cow *(right)* turns its head to a three-quarter view, the muzzle narrows down and the eye assumes a tear-drop shape.

Seen in side view *(left)*, the alignment of eye and nostril is similar to that in the three-quarter view – but now the eye is round.

1 This diagrammatic rendering of a calf's head shows it in terms of the most basic shapes, with lines to link the features *(above)*. Notice how, due to perspective, the ear on the far side is higher, and how the muzzle below the nostrils is foreshortened.

2 The finished drawing, still with some construction lines to show the alignment of key features *(above right)*.

Artist's Tip

You can sometimes buy quite good little models of farm animals, and these can be very useful to work from to improve your knowledge of proportion and perspective.

Viewed from a rear three-quarter view, this calf's muzzle is foreshortened *(right)*. The relative sizes of ears and eyes tell us that it is a young animal.

Proportions of birds

As with farm mammals, the proportions of farm birds vary depending on the bird's age and the observer's viewpoint. For example, the Khaki-Campbell duck on the right is full-grown, and its wings and body have reached full length. Its head and feet are smaller in proportion to its size than those of the ducklings below.

A side view of the characterful Muscovy duck is shown opposite. The relative proportions of head to body are shown in superimposed rectangles. The body itself suggests a cone shape with the sharp end at the tail, and, from side view, the facial features are not distorted.

As the same bird walks towards us, however, its cone-shaped body changes to become almost circular. We are looking along the face, which therefore shows the effect of foreshortening.

The structure of the body is very obvious in young birds *(below)*. It is the heads and feet which enlarge least as they grow.

As the same birds mature, the body grows larger, making the head and feet look proportionately smaller *(above)*.

Artist's Tip

In side view, ducks' bodies have an underlying 'S' shape. The 'S' shape is more rounded in young birds.

1 & 2 From the front, the shape of the duck's body can be broken down into concentric circles *(right)*. The crop and breast conceal the wings and tail behind. As we look along the length of the duck's paddle-feet, they become narrower.

1 & 2 You can judge the relative proportions of head to body by casting imaginary rectangles around them. Note that most of the body is ahead of the legs. Proportions of eye to beak to head should be kept in mind to capture the character of this duck.

Looking at Features

Once you have learned about the broad outlines of farm animals, it is time to look more closely at their features – noses, ears, beaks, feet, etc.

Farm mammals
The eating habits of farm mammals affect the shape of their features. The cow has a wide muzzle to accommodate the large tongue which crops the grass. The jaws of sheep are smaller, as are the nostrils which fit neatly over the mouth-parts rather like a hare. As in many grazing animals, the eye is large and placed high on the head to keep a look-out for danger.

The pig eats anything available. Its upper lip curls slightly over its upper canine, and the nostrils are circular, with a sharper upper edge; the lower edge is moist and slightly shiny.

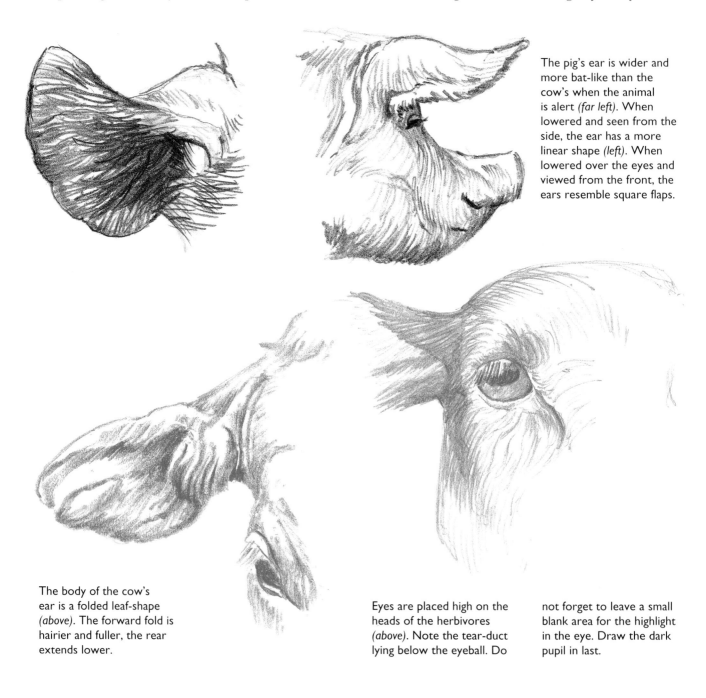

The pig's ear is wider and more bat-like than the cow's when the animal is alert *(far left)*. When lowered and seen from the side, the ear has a more linear shape *(left)*. When lowered over the eyes and viewed from the front, the ears resemble square flaps.

The body of the cow's ear is a folded leaf-shape *(above)*. The forward fold is hairier and fuller, the rear extends lower.

Eyes are placed high on the heads of the herbivores *(above)*. Note the tear-duct lying below the eyeball. Do not forget to leave a small blank area for the highlight in the eye. Draw the dark pupil in last.

The sheep's nose is more pointed than the cow's, and the nostrils are closer together, having a narrower tear-drop shape *(above)*. The division in the middle of the upper lip is also more visible.

The pig's snout is made for rootling and pushing through soil and this is reflected in its shape *(above)*. The flat 'pushing' end, which has almost an upside-down heart shape, is backed by circular folds of flesh that give the snout its flexibility.

I The cow's muzzle is box-like and extends round into the fleshy upper jaw *(right)*. Two tear-drop shapes curling towards each other sum up the basis for the nostrils. They narrow into the rising 'V' on the bridge of the nose. Being a bulky animal, the cow can open its nostrils wider to inhale more air when it exerts itself.

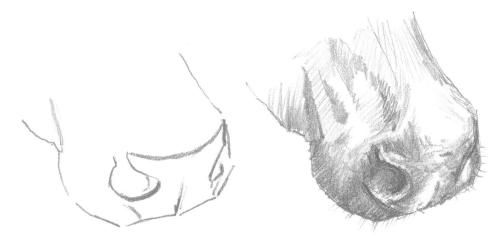

2 The cow's nose is damp and thus shiny, so remember to leave unmarked paper areas for highlights facing the light direction. The deeper tones inside the nostrils will need more pressure and a softer pencil.

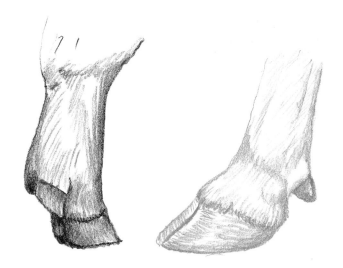

Pig's trotters lift the animal off the ground slightly *(far left)*. This gives the animal a springy walk.

The cow's cloven foot rests firmly on the ground *(left)*. As weight is put on to it, it splays somewhat. The redundant toes on both cows and pigs are placed up behind the foot, out of the way.

Farm birds

The red comb and wattles (the flap below the chin) are among the most familiar features of farmyard cockerels and hens, a signal to their companions of their relative health, and their status in the flock. The comb flares back from the beak, sometimes covering it; the wattles begin below the bill and extend past the eye, and the plumage flows from these down the nape and neck. The heads and eyes of these birds are not large – the eye is emphasized by a number of fleshy rings around it.

The cockerel's legs and feet are powerful, and plated with scales. This protects them from thorns in scrub where they scratch and search for food. The three-toed arrangement acts like a spreading stand, enabling the bird to rest easily on one leg.

The duck has a similar arrangement of toes, but webbing has evolved between them. Ducks waddle on land, but on water they float easily, propelled by these paddles. The toes are thinner than those of the cockerel and hen.

This chick has not grown adult features *(above)*. The eye appears nearer the bill, which is small.

Here *(above)* the artist has used a textured paper and soft pencil to work into the cockerel's comb. The pencil marks for feathers sweep back from it.

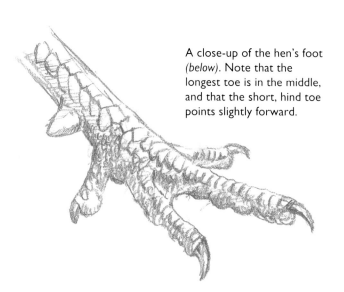

A close-up of the hen's foot *(below)*. Note that the longest toe is in the middle, and that the short, hind toe points slightly forward.

The duck's foot is similar in arrangement to the hen's, but the rear claw is undeveloped *(above)*.

Look for simple forms, such as triangles, rectangles and squares, as you draw the drake's tail *(right)*.

Feathers

Feather detail forms an important feature of farmyard birds. For example, the curly feathers that complete the rhythmic pattern of the drake's plumage have evolved from the upper tail coverts, supported by the tail. The tail itself is formed by overlapping, fan-like feathers.

In the case of the cockerel, the bird's 'sickles' are not tail feathers either but, like those of the drake, are highly evolved upper tail coverts which are supported by the tail itself. These sickles radiate out from the tail area, and wind and gravity twist and bend their shapes into visually exciting patterns.

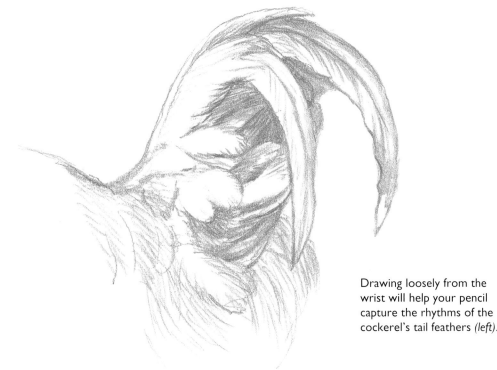

Drawing loosely from the wrist will help your pencil capture the rhythms of the cockerel's tail feathers *(left)*.

Artist's Tip

You do not always need to keep your pencils sharpened to a fine point. Use the bluntness of soft pencil work to convey the softness of feathers or fur.

41

Light and Shade

When you understand the principles of light and shade, your drawings of farm animals will become more convincingly three-dimensional.

When light falls on the animals' bodies, the parts nearest the light will be the brightest. As the light glances away, over and under the body, the surfaces become darker in tone. When the light is overhead, the darkest areas are under the body; when it comes from the side, both top and underneath will be deeper in tone.

Light direction
When you begin, observe your subject to see which direction the light is mainly coming from – bearing in mind that it may come from more than one direction.

The irregular surface of fur or feathers can, however, create complicated patterns of light and shade, but with practice you will soon learn to pick out the main masses that are highlighted or in shadow.

Although sketchy in quality, this drawing still conveys the broad masses of light and dark.

The massive shape of the bull *(right)* is a good subject for the study of shadow. I blocked out the main areas of light and shade, then hatched in pencil strokes for the middle tones and overlapped the strokes for the darkest. I left the upper areas untouched to suggest light on the form. The bull's head casts its own shadow on the neck.

Artist's Tip

Place a spherical object, such as an apple or orange, next to a direct light source, such as a table lamp, and study how the light affects it. You will find that the shadow often appears deepest where light and shade meet.

1 Draw in the outline of your hen lightly to suggest the main masses *(right)*.

2 Decide what direction the light is coming from – then begin to shade in these masses *(far right)*.

Texture and Pattern

As well as the differences in their overall shape, farm animals also have a variety of surface texture and pattern – think of the smooth, velvety quality of a horse's coat with its soft sheen, the matt, rough texture of sheep's wool, and the wonderful feather patterns and textures of hens and ducks.

Fur and feathers
All of these qualities can be expressed in different combinations of media and surface – the trick is to choose the combination which produces the quality you want most effectively.

The softness of sheep's wool might be conveyed by a medium that has a 'blurry' quality, such as charcoal, for example; the effect can be increased if this is used on a slightly rough surface. The bold stripes and patches on feathers could be well expressed by a medium that produces clean lines, such as pencil or felt-tip pen, applied to a relatively smooth surface.

The feather patterns of these turkeys (above) make a decorative pattern like a sunburst of marks radiating out from a centre. The wax crayon used makes a vital and decisive mark.

In this drawing of a sheep *(right)*, the artist has painted loosely on to rough watercolour paper and then worked over it with crayon and ink. He has deepened the background texture and allowed the sheep to emerge from it, keeping the white shafts of light on the wool clean.

In this drawing of a Tamworth pig *(left)*, the artist has used sweeping strokes of the pencil, on its side or its point, with varying pressure, to convey the coarse hairiness of the animal's coat.

Working in detail

Rough paper and the texture of charcoal pencil or chalk can be the means to make close studies of widely diverse animals.

In the study of a bull's head below, the overall rough texture suggests the animal's craggy form, and this overall quality unifies the details. The artist has carefully rendered the curly forelock, the fine hair around the nostrils, and the skin texture of the muzzle. He has held back from working too heavily into the forehead and nasal bridge to preserve their light tone. The horns are shiny with a line of highlight along them. The ears are hairy and dark and thus absorb light.

Another interesting alternative when conveying texture and pattern is to draw 'in reverse' using a light medium that is capable of making marks on a dark background. In the drawing opposite, the soft pastel has captured the patterns and highlights of the turkey's glossy feather masses.

Artist's Tip

Always have a range of papers, colours and surfaces available so that you can try out different media on them to see what textures they produce.

Here *(right)* the artist has been sensitive to the different textures of skin and hair, and has varied the use of his pencil accordingly.

This drawing has been produced in white pastel on black sugar paper *(right)*. The image could first be sketched out in a darker medium such as pencil.

Behaviour and Movement

Most farm animals live in herds or flocks; they are social and do things together. Although they are social creatures, this does not mean that they all have the same status. For example, a single cockerel will be dominant in the poultry flock, and his favourite hen will dominate the other hens – a position often ruthlessly maintained.

Maternal behaviour
To counteract this aggression, the relationship between parent and offspring is a touching sight that immediately appeals to the artist, as in the drawing of the long-legged foal feeding from its mother opposite.

The 'broody' mother hen is a particularly powerful symbol of maternal care. When she broods her chicks, she keeps them on her brood patch, fluffing out her feathers over them. They will shelter under her at night, or run to her in the day. As she feeds, she will keep an eye on them, over her shoulder.

Feeding habits
Knowing something of cows' biology will help you understand their behaviour. When they lie down to 'ruminate', for example, they are re-chewing the grass they have cropped in order to digest it.

In their various activities, cows tend to gather together, lying down for shade or rest. Here a small group of cows ruminates. I did this study in dilute Indian ink and a no. 4 brush which gives a nice point.

Artist's Tip

When you are observing animal behaviour, approach the animals gently and without noise. They will become less afraid and more inquisitive if you avoid eye-contact.

Observation and knowledge of light and shadow can help you put down an image quickly. Here *(above)* a Suffolk Punch foal feeds from its mother.

I had a photograph of some chicks which helped me visualize this image *(right)* which I had seen many times without actually drawing the scene.

The cockerel advertises its presence by crowing loudly *(left)*. The effort involved forces the cockerel to stretch its body, curve its neck and open its beak.

Soft pencil on cartridge paper is the best way to capture the quick movements of preening breeds *(above)*. The feathers spread like petals from a flower.

Artist's Tip

Sometimes rapid movement defeats the eye. A mark or two and a squiggle can be built up later from your knowledge of the animals' forms.

Although the head has disappeared, the small feathers and the direction of feet give clues to this preening hen's pose *(above)*.

Geese are good sentinels *(left)*; they make cackling calls and hissing noises when alarmed. This is accompanied by the exciting serpentine shapes of their threat postures.

Animals in motion

The commotion illustrated below can happen suddenly; the piglets may be feeding quietly and then take it into their heads to stampede. When they run, their front and back legs stretch apart and close together in unison. When walking, the legs on one side close up, while on the other side they spread apart so that a sort of tripod effect constantly supports the body.

The panicking hens have lowered their heads, and the stretched angle of the legs is exaggerated. The feet appear to have left the ground because the shadow has been sketched in a few strokes below them.

The few static items – straw, pitchfork, and brickwork – provide a striking contrast that serves to emphasize the animals' movement.

A rich black wax pencil was used here. I sketched and traced out the drawing many times before I was satisfied with the composition.

Sketching

Sketching is the lifeblood of the animal artist's work. The pencil on the page will follow your watchful eye as it observes what is going on in the farmyard. Noting what you see will add to your growing store of information for more ambitious work such as painting and sculpture.

Making a start
Where do you begin? First, get yourself a sketchbook – the hardback type with paper that can take a wash of paint for colour-notes – and a soft pencil that will move swiftly and easily over the paper. Thus equipped, start by making mental notes on the animals and the general activity. Then, when you are ready, choose a particular subject to draw, and work fast; don't worry in the least if your sketch doesn't look 'right' – you can expand it when you get home.

As time goes on, your sketches will improve, and you will possess your own library, chock-full of all the animals you have recorded.

A sketch, improved at home, of two significant positions in feeding cows *(left)*. The cows make simple rectangular shapes.

The effect of light and shade, captured with charcoal on cartridge paper – a sketch which will make a good basis for a more finished composition later *(right)*. The dark background highlights the cow.

The artist looked for the simplest shapes when drawing these cows *(above)*.

Bold pencil strokes, at different angles, convey the roughness of this Jacob's sheep's fleece *(below)*.

The folded limbs and relaxed attitude of this bullock suggest peaceful rumination *(above)*.

Any line was better than none as I tried to capture the feeling of massiveness in this bull's head and neck *(above* and *above right)*.

Artist's Tip

Do not get too anxious when you begin sketching. Relax, take in the atmosphere and observe the animals before you start.

Visual reminder

Sketching is a means to aid your memory – what pigs' ears look like from diverse angles, the arch of a crowing cock's neck, or lambs climbing on their feeder. Your sketchbook is private, for your eyes only. It does not matter if your note is just a squiggle: it may be just what you need later for a detailed drawing or composition.

The important thing is to note your observation as soon as possible. Constant practice means improvement. You will find that your visual memory improves and you remember much more than you actually draw.

Suitable materials

You can sketch with a pencil, ballpoint, or felt-tip – whatever you feel at home with. You can take with you large pieces of paper on a board, a tiny notepad and clutch-pencil tucked in your top pocket, or a combination of them all.

The positions of the hens' feet fascinated me (*above* and *right*), as did the shapes of the birds themselves.

These sketches of pigs' heads (*left, above* and *below*) are no more than a few lines, yet contain essential information. The full figure (*right*) records the form and markings.

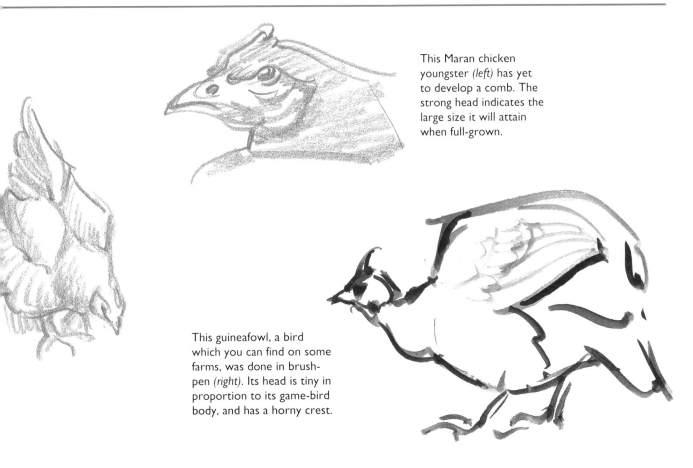

This Maran chicken youngster *(left)* has yet to develop a comb. The strong head indicates the large size it will attain when full-grown.

This guineafowl, a bird which you can find on some farms, was done in brush-pen *(right)*. Its head is tiny in proportion to its game-bird body, and has a horny crest.

Artist's Tip

Attract poultry with a handful of grain. They move quickly, but all your squiggles will capture movement and add to your knowledge.

Using pencil and wash, the artist here has noted the bow-shaped resting cockerel, and the upright tails of the chickens *(left)*.

In Setting

When placing your farmyard animals in a setting, it is always tempting to include too much surrounding paraphenalia – but avoid this temptation. A mass of details can distract from the animal or bird which is your main subject.

Setting the scene
Think of the scene as a stage setting, in which just a few clues may be enough to create a sense of place. A single bucket or fence-post, for example, will convey a farmyard setting.

In this drawing, I varied the tones and the weight of line to separate the various elements that make up the whole. Notice, for example, how I used a dark line along the sow's back to separate her from the fence, and visually to bring her body forwards in the space.

Choosing what to include
When creating a setting, try to include 'working' details only, that provide useful information and contribute to the composition. In the drawing below, the perspective of the bars on the gate as they spread out towards us tells us that we are looking down on the animals, while implying space in the foreground in which they can move about – piglets are always restless. A few pencil marks on the ground suggest wisps of straw, in contrast to the bold uprights of the fence which are strong enough to contain the sow's bulk.

The drinking basin in the foreground echoes the sow's shape, and draws the eye in. Including such authentic details shows that the artist has looked carefully at the scene.

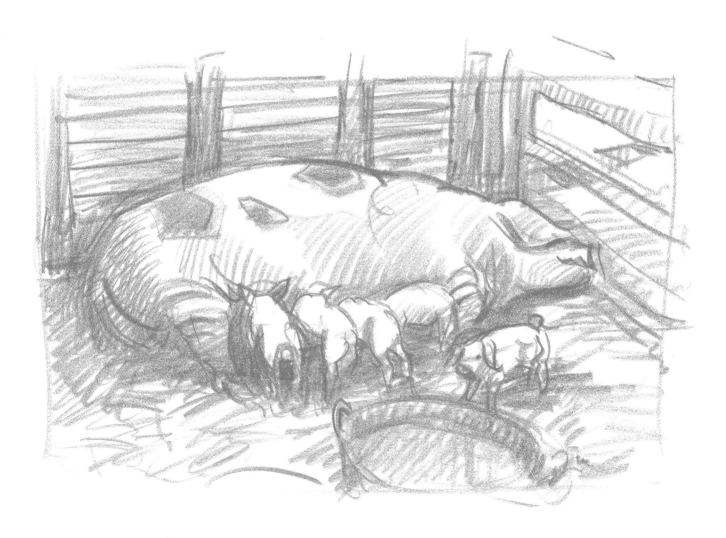

Mood and time

As well as giving a sense of physical place, situating an animal in a setting can also be a way of conveying a particular mood, time, or event. For example, including just a simple shadow may be enough to suggest light direction, time of day, and weather conditions.

Drawings of mother animals with their young create a powerful sense of place and time, and may need little additional detail. In the two drawings on this page, the only hint of physical surroundings are a few wispy lines to suggest straw and shadow.

Here *(above)*, the artist has captured the relationship between mother and calf – both shapes echo each other. Interest is provided by the textures of hair and straw, drawn with a clutch pencil. This gives a fine line without the need for constant sharpening.

I used a soft 8B pencil to produce these sketches of a ewe and her lamb *(right)*. The lamb had just been born and lay prone for a while, but within an hour it was tottering around after its mother.

I was careful not to disturb these ducks *(left)* and was thus able to capture their sleeping forms snuggled into the grass, which is suggested by a few sketchy lines.

such as stables, or even the farms where animals are gathered for exhibition and competition, provide a fascinating backdrop for your animals.

The Aylesbury ducks on the left are enjoying a rest on the grass, their two bodies echoing each other. Below left, two bantams work around a feeder. Below right, the hen with her chicks looks relaxed and safe amongst the straw, while the chick shares the food with its mother. The small, intimate details in such drawings do much to convey a sense of mood and setting.

Working from sketches

All the close-up studies of farm birds on this page began life as notes put down speedily for later information.

Adding small authentic items such as drinking and food bowls around which the animals gather can build a sketch up into a scene. Larger areas

A quick sketch of two hens pecking at a feeder *(above)* conjures in the mind a much wider farmyard scene.

This sketch was done with a clutch-type pencil – the artist strengthened the drawing later *(above)*.

This sketch of feeding time for the huge Suffolk Punch horses *(above)* was done on the spot. I added to it later.

Agricultural shows provide excellent opportunities for gathering information. This quick pencil study of people and animals *(right)* was done at one such show, where some fine examples were being judged.

Framing and Composition

Framing refers to the size and proportions of the paper or surface you choose to work within. You do not need to accept the sizes provided by the manufacturers. You can select any section from your picture, vertical or horizontal. It may vastly improve your composition.

Composition is about arranging the elements you want to use in your picture to maximum effect. It may take some thought and many small sketches to decide what will work best. You will be looking to create mood, atmosphere and meaning.

Deciding on a composition
When you get down to the design, ask yourself what person, animal or thing is most important to the picture and how you can bring this out.

You may find that you have – reluctantly – to leave out some favourite item that does not contribute to the main theme. Never mind; this can start off a new picture!

Try out different media in your preparatory drawings, too. Does the subject suggest charcoal, or pencil? Does it demand pen and ink, or coloured wax pencils?

Two examples
In the light-hearted composition of sheep blocking a country lane here, I have tackled the scene from two angles – one a low viewpoint, the other higher. In the smaller sketch, the shepherd's figure is larger. This could be further enhanced by framing down – reducing the area around him, even cropping out part of the car.

This is a working sketch, much rubbed out, altered and re-drawn. The sketches of the little car were done at a rally. Soft pencil is the quickest means of doing thumbnail sketches.

Scale and balance

In the first small sketch, the figure and car dominate the scene – they are bigger and the light falls behind them. The sheep are about to surround the viewer. In the second, larger drawing, I have allowed space for the sheep to move into. The shepherd emerges from the shady lane into the light, and the car is almost concealed, only to be noticed later.

Remember to keep your composition simple. Avoid placing your important figures slap in the middle; place them to the side and above the middle to avoid predictability.

This piece was done on tinted paper with pen and wash. A little white was added for highlights on the foliage. It is always best to work lightly to begin with and steadily deepen lines and tones as necessary.

Artist's Tip

As you work across your drawing adding tone and detail, use a piece of paper under your hand to avoid greasing or smudging work you have already done.

Working from Photos

Artists have always made use of photographs, and film and video can provide the animal artist with more information than ever before.

Using the camera

I always carry a still camera with me on my trips, but use it mostly for recording background detail: I never rely on the camera entirely and always sketch as well. Photographs offer us only one small moment in time, whereas sketches can capture movement, space and continuity, as our eyes scan the whole scene.

If you want to sketch in comfort, television films and programmes, recorded on video, provide the ideal opportunity. Although both camera and animal move, the freeze-frame facility will allow you to stop the film to do your drawing.

Highland cattle have a distinctive appearance, but are not that easy to find, so a photograph *(above)* provides a useful reference. I began by doing a fairly literal copy of the photograph *(above right)*, paying particular attention to areas of light and shade.

In my second attempt, I focused on one area of the animal around the head and shoulder *(right)*. Fading out at the edges, the drawing makes a pleasing arrangement, no longer confined by the rectangle of the original image.

A starting point

We do not have to be slaves to the photograph: it can be a departure point for a range of approaches. You can, for example, combine images from different photographs in one composition. Alternatively, if the arrangement of items in the photograph doesn't work as well as it might, you can always leave out, or add, a particular element when doing your drawing.

Remember, a photograph or video picture is merely a visual aid. Avoid copying it slavishly, and your drawing will be much more lively.

To achieve my final drawing, I used the animal from the photograph, but built in other elements to add interest and balance to the composition – there are now two Highland cattle grazing in a field, with a line of trees behind. Note the interplay of light and dark areas, and how these make the drawing easier to 'read'.